THE FAME GAME
A PLAY
Tony Norman

Illustrated by Graham Smith

Titles in First Flight

Phantom Striker
Pest Control
Shark's Fin Island
Scary!
Ping Pong with King Kong
The Fame Game
Awesome Animals
Big, Fast Rides
Car Boot Genie
Monster Cards
Ssh! My Family are Spies
Ghost Dog Mystery
Chip Boy
Sky Bikers
Surfing Three-Sixty
Something in the Kitchen
The Ghost in the Art Room
Robert and the Werewolf
The Biggest Lies Ever
Mad about Money

Badger Publishing Limited
Oldmedow Road, Hardwick Industrial Estate,
Kings Lynn PE30 4JJ
Telephone: 01438 791037
www.badgerlearning.co.uk

2 4 6 8 10 9 7 5 3 1

The Fame Game A Play ISBN 1 84424 822 3

First edition © 2006
This second edition © 2013

Text © Tony Norman 2006
Complete work © Badger Publishing Limited 2006

All rights reserved. No part of this publication may be reproduced, stored in any form or by any means mechanical, electronic, recording or otherwise without the prior permission of the publisher.

The right of Tony Norman to be identified as author of this Work has been asserted by him in accordance with the Copyright, Designs and Patents Act 1988.

Series Editor: Jonny Zucker
Publisher: David Jamieson
Commissioning Editor: Carrie Lewis
Editor: Paul Martin
Design: Fiona Grant
Illustration: Graham Smith

THE FAME GAME
A PLAY
Tony Norman

Contents

Characters **4**
Scene 1 Drama Club **6**
Scene 2 Ad-Lib **11**
Scene 3 The Fame Game **17**
Scene 4 Zak's TV Show **19**
Scene 5 The Last Word **28**

Characters

Hailey – Wants to be a rap star

Sarah – Dreams of being a top model

Mrs Abrey – Drama Club teacher

Zak – A show-off! Plays a TV chat show host

Matt – Lives football, sleeps football

Scene 1 Drama Club

Lunch break at Red Oak School. Four members of the Drama Club are waiting for their teacher to arrive...

Zak:
You liked it?

Hailey:
Yes.

Sarah:
So what?

Matt:
I like pasta too. I eat pasta before a game.

Zak:
That wasn't pasta, Matt.

Sarah:
What was it then?

Zak:
It was green and smelly.

Hailey:
Sounds like you, Zak.

Sarah *(laughing)*:
Good one, Hailey.

Zak:
It's no joke Sarah. We could all have been poisoned!

Zak falls to the floor and starts groaning.

Matt *(football commentator's voice)*:
And the full-time score here at Red Oak Primary is... Pasta one, Zak nil.

Mrs Abrey, the drama teacher, walks in.

Mrs Abrey:
Are you ill, Zak?

Sarah:
He's acting the fool…

Sarah and Hailey:
… as usual!

Mrs Abrey:
Why don't we all do some acting?

Matt:
Yeah, come on you lot. We'll be in extra time soon!

Zak:
Okay. I'll show you how it's done.

Zak gets up. The kids gather round Mrs Abrey.

Scene 2 Ad-Lib

Mrs Abrey:
Today we are going to ad-lib a drama. Do you know what that means?

Hailey:
It means we don't have to learn the words!

Mrs Abrey:
That's right. You make up the play as you go along.

Sarah:
Cool.

Matt:
I'll take each line as it comes.

Hailey:
What is the play about?

Mrs Abrey:
Let's play 'The Fame Game!' Who wants to be a star?

Hailey, Sarah, Zak and Matt *(loudly)*:
ME!!!

Mrs Abrey:
And what's so good about being a star?

Zak:
You make lots of money, so you can buy what you like.

Matt:
Yeah, I'd buy a big house with my own football pitch in the garden.

Sarah:
I'd fly to New York and buy loads of new clothes.

Hailey:
I'd like a big flashy car.

Sarah:
You can't drive.

Zak:
Yes she can. She drives me up the wall.

Hailey (*bored voice*)**:**
Very funny Zak.

Zak (*laughs*)**:**
Thanks Hailey.

Mrs Abrey:
Okay now, stars have lots of money, they drive fast cars and fly all over the world. Do you think it's a good life?

Hailey:
Very good.

Sarah:
The best.

Mrs Abrey:
But do bad things come with fame, too?

Zak:
No way.

Hailey:
I hate to say this, but Zak's right.

Scene 3 The Fame Game

Mrs Abrey:
So, what kind of star do you want to be?

Matt:
A football star.

Sarah:
A model.

Hailey (*rap voice*):
I'm a girl who will go far,
I'm gonna be a big rap star!

Zak:
And I want to be a TV star with my own chat show. You lot can be on it if you like.

Mrs Abrey:
That's a good idea.

Sarah:
A rapper, a top model and a football star...

Matt:
The dream team...

Zak:
All on my TV show. I like it!

Scene 4 Zak's TV Show

Hailey, Sarah and Matt sit in a line on three chairs. Zak stands and pretends to talk to a TV camera.

Zak *(big smile):*
Hello. This is Zak's TV Show. What is it really like to be famous? Let's ask my three star guests tonight.

Zak sits down and turns to Matt.

Zak:
Matt, you are a top football star. What do you like most about being famous?

Matt:
Playing football.

Zak:
But what do you do when you go out?

Matt:
I don't go out much, because fans know my face and follow me.

Zak:
So you stay home. What do you do there?

Matt:
I like TV.

Zak:
What do you watch?

Matt:
Football.

Zak:
You must like other shows, too.

Matt:
Yes, at half-time I turn over and watch pop videos for a bit.

Zak:
Then what?

Matt:
Then I turn back to the football.

Zak:
Football… Football… That's all you talk about. Don't you ever get sick of it?

Matt:
No Zak, I'm over the moon!

Zak turns to Sarah.

Zak:
Sarah, as a top model you travel the world. Do you like eating out?

Sarah:
Yes, I've met some of the best chefs in the world.

Zak:
New York, Paris, London, Rome, you've been to them all. Which city has the best food?

Sarah:
I don't know really.

Zak:
Why?

Sarah:
Well, because I always have salad and a glass of water.

Zak:
Then what?

Sarah:
Then I go to bed early, so I look my best the next day.

Zak:
Newsflash Sarah… your life is boring!

Hailey:
You're the one who is boring, Zak. I'm taking over!

Hailey jumps to her feet and starts rapping.

Hailey:
There's a TV star –
and this is a fact,
He's very boring – his name is Zak.
He loves the sound –
of his own voice,
So turn him off –
you have the choice.

I'm Hailey the rapper –
and this I know,
Zak's TV Show has got to go!

Sarah and Matt laugh and clap their hands. Zak looks angry.

Scene 5 The Last Word

Zak jumps up and starts shouting at Hailey.

Zak:
You can't say things like that.

Hailey:
I'm a cool rapper. I say what I like.

Zak:
And what if nobody buys your next song, how many fans will you have then?

Hailey:
More than you, you dweeb!

Mrs Abrey:
Okay, okay, just stop that you two.

Zak and Hailey glare at each other.

Now, what did ad-libbing that play tell you about 'The Fame Game'?

Matt:
Big stars have to hide to get away from people.

Sarah:
Models are always on a diet.

Hailey:
Rap stars need hit records.

Zak:
Or they become losers... like Hailey!

Hailey pulls a face at Zak. Zak grins.

Mrs Abrey:
Okay, there is one last question. Now you have seen how hard it is to be a star, do you still want to be famous?

Hailey, Sarah, Zak and Matt *(loudly)*:
YES!!